The Loss of a Loved One

A Teen's Guide to coping and healing

DEDICATION

You know how it is. You pick up a book, flip to the dedication, and find that, once again, the author has dedicated a book to someone else and not to you.

Not this time.

Because we haven't yet met/have only a glancing acquaintance, or haven't seen each other in much too long/are in some way related/will never meet, but will, I trust, despite that, always think fondly of each other...

This one's for you.

You are doing great, you are strong, I am proud to know you!

TABLE OF CONTENTS

INTRODUCTION

Although it is never easy to lose a loved one or be surrounded by them in so many aspects of their lives, the impact on a teenager dependent on them can be even more devastating. Teens are often left to deal with funeral arrangements and grief following the death of a parent or grandparent.

Teens can feel resentful after the death of a family member.

The teenage years can be very exciting but also incredibly difficult. It cannot be easy to lose someone you love. It can feel like the world has collapsed around you. You might feel isolated, especially if you are young.

Too many teenagers live with the grief and death that comes with it.

Today's high school students will have lost 5 percent of their parents by graduation, while 20 percent will have witnessed the death of a close relative by age 18. 91% of respondents said they had experienced the death or loss of a family member.

COMMON REACTIONS OF GRIEVING TEENS

While grief is unique to each person, some reactions are common and accepted as normal. These are the most common feelings or behaviors that teens experience after a family member's death.

- A feeling of empty stomach and loss of appetite.
- Guilt about something said or done, or something left unsaid.
- Anger and lashing out at other people, sometimes for no reason.
- Anger at the dead for their death, followed by guilt.
- The smallest things can affect mood.
- Unexpected crying or outbursts
- Feel that you cannot concentrate on the task at hand and restlessness.
- Sensing the presence of the deceased, expecting him or her to enter the door at the normal time, hearing their voice, or feeling that they are "seeing" them out of their corner.
- Talking about pictures
- Conversations with the dead in a special location
- Troubled dreams or sleeplessness
- You may adopt the mannerisms or traits of the deceased or wear clothes familiar to them.

- Teens can experience emotional regression or even bed-wetting.
- The need to tell and recall stories about a loved one to the point that it becomes a burden for others.
- A failure to communicate or a need to be responsible.
- Assume the role of the "new" household member, taking care of everyone else and distracting from their own emotions.

There are many ways to lose a friend or loved one when you're a teenager. This book will provide some information and help you get through the grieving process. This book offers tips and information to help teens cope with the loss. It also discusses the various stages of grief.

UNDERSTANDING GRIEF

Grief refers to the profound sadness and loss you feel after someone you love dies. Losing a loved one could bring about a significant change in your life. It can take time to grieve and to find ways to adjust. As you grieve, comfort and support can be a great help.

In her 1969 book On Death and Dying, Elisabeth Kubler–Ross outlined grief's five stages. Grief is often thought of as a response to death. However, it can also occur when the reality is not what we expected or desired.

Persistent, traumatic grief may cause us to go through the stages of grief, sometimes very quickly: denial, anger, bargaining, depression, and acceptance. These are our attempts at coping with change and protecting ourselves as we adjust to a new reality. Although each stage has common elements, grieving is different for everyone.

It is overwhelming to combine trauma and stress with grief. It can have a devastating effect on our mental and bodily health. The stress response is a nervous system reaction to feeling threatened. It impacts our minds and bodies. This triggers adrenaline and cortisol release, which can impact sleep and appetite, making it difficult for you to function at your best.

Anxiety and depression symptoms can develop along with trauma symptoms such as intrusive thoughts or nightmares. Trauma resulting from racial injustice can be chronic. Here are resources for Black healing.

Understanding the stages of grief and how you experience them can help increase compassion and self-understanding. This can help you better understand your needs and prioritize the tasks that will meet them.

Stage 1: Denial

Can look like

- Avoidance
- Procrastination
- Forgetting
- Easily distracted
- Mindless behaviors
- Keeping busy all the time
- Thinking/saying, "I'm fine" or "it's fine."

Stage 2: Anger

Can Look Like

- Pessimism
- Cynicism
- Sarcasm
- Irritability
- Being aggressive or passive-aggressive
- Getting into arguments or physical fights
- Increased alcohol or drug use

Stage 3: Bargaining

Can look like

- Ruminating on the future or past
- Over-thinking and worrying
- Comparing self to others
- Predicting the future and assuming the worst
- Perfectionism
- Thinking/saying, "I should have…" or "if only…."
- Judgment toward self and others

Stage 4: Depression

Can look like

- Sleep and appetite changes
- Reduced energy
- Reduced social interest
- Reduced motivation
- Crying, disappointment
- Increased alcohol or drug use

Stage 5: Acceptance

Can look like

- Mindful behaviors
- Engaging with reality as it is
- "This is how it is right now."
- Being present in the moment
- Able to be vulnerable & tolerate emotions
- Assertive, non-defensive, honest communication
- Adapting, coping, and responding skillfully

Acceptance is a state of mind we must reach if we want to accept reality. You might find yourself sleeping more. Perhaps our moods or anxiety can become the main focus of attention and distract from external stressors. To avoid reality or disconnect from it, we might resort to drugs or alcohol. We might focus on our tasks, responsibilities, or needs to avoid distress.

Acceptance does not mean you will never experience distress, emotions, or trauma. Acceptance does not mean that you accept what is happening. This means being aware of what you are fighting for, validating your desire against it, and reorienting to the present moment. This means not getting stuck or being unstuck from other stages. Mindfulness and a curious, non-judgmental attitude can help tremendously.

Acceptance could look like you saying to yourself, "If I sleep too much today, I'll continue sleeping through the night." I will prioritize getting my schedule in order." This might be like noting that you are directing your anger and sadness at yourself and dwelling on your mistakes. I will acknowledge my anger and the real reason for it." Or, you might reflect on what I could be mad about. It's natural to be anxious about _____. It's not easy to accept that ___ is there. You might try this: "If my needs are neglected, and I focus on other people, I'll feel burned out and exhausted." I will take the time to evaluate how I am doing and what I need.

It is uncommon to go through each stage in a straight line. It is normal for people to feel mood swings and changes in thoughts, attitudes, or behaviors. Sometimes it can be hard to accept things that seem so unacceptable.

WHAT CAN GRIEF DO TO YOU?

How grief affects, you will depend on how close you were to the deceased. It all depends on how important the deceased person was in your life. Losing a sibling, parent, grandparent, or close friend can be more difficult.

The circumstances of the death can also affect how grief affects you. The sudden loss, suicide, and violence of a loved one can make grief more severe. A person may require additional support to heal after the death of a close friend or family member.

Sometimes, the intensity of grief is greatest soon after someone dies. Some people may not feel their grief immediately. Some people may feel disbelief, shock, or numbness. It's okay to feel that way. It may take some time before it sinks in that the person has passed.

You might be experiencing grief.

Grief can affect your feelings.

There are likely to be many emotions. You may feel different emotions every day. Sometimes you may feel sad, angry, anxious, or guilty. Other times, you may feel love, gratitude, or tenderness.

Be aware of how your emotions change and are open to them. Instead of trying to change how you feel, accept what you are feeling. Talking about your feelings with someone you trust can be helpful. It is also helpful to notice the good things that occur during sad times and losses, even the small ones.

Grief can affect your thoughts.

It might be a good idea to reflect on the times you shared with your loved ones. There are many things that you regret or you might be worried about. You might imagine what your life would be without them. You might consider what the person meant to you.

Pay attention to the thoughts that come and then go. You might find it helpful to share your thoughts. Write a letter or journal to your loved one. You can use this to thank them for being a part of your life, express your feelings, and say what you wish they had said. You should allow yourself to reflect and think and give yourself breaks when needed.

Grief can affect your body.

You may experience sleep or appetite problems due to grief. You may feel more tired or have less energy than normal. You might feel restless or tired. It might not be easy to relax or concentrate. A "heaviness" or "tightness" may be felt in the chest, stomach, or stomach. It cannot be easy to lose a loved one. Stress can also have temporary effects on your health.

Pay attention to how grief affects you. Get the rest, nutrition, and exercise you need. Mindful breathing can be a helpful practice.

Grief may lead you to ask difficult questions.

Many ask, "Why did this happen?" and "What happens when people die?" Others question their religious beliefs. Some people find strength in their faith. Others discover spiritual connections. Others find people they are closer to in their lives.

Big questions can lead to new insights. You can find meaning and purpose in grief. You might find it helpful to reflect on your life and what is most important to you. Many people find it useful to write down these thoughts or reflect on them in a journal.

HOW LONG DO YOU GRIEVE?

There is no time frame for grieving. It is okay to feel grief for weeks or months.

People often gather together to support and comfort one another in the days or weeks following the death of a loved one. They attend funerals and memorial services. They spend time talking to each other and sharing their memories of the deceased. They may bring food or cards.

People may think they can get over their grief when they return to normal life. They may find it difficult to give their best effort in everyday life for a time. They still feel grief, even though they don't talk as often about the loss.

As time passes, grief changes and becomes less intense. Many people feel grief in "waves," which can come and go. Sometimes, a reminder of a loved person can trigger a strong wave of grief. Sometimes, the grief is forgotten and can fade into the background of their daily activities.

WHEN WILL I FEEL BETTER?

It's normal to feel and ask questions after the death of someone you love. It is normal to start to feel better. Usually, feeling better happens slowly.

The amount of grief you feel or the length of it does not measure how much you love the person. Not feeling better does not mean you should forget about your loved one or get over them.

You may find that your grief is slowly fading, and you realize how much the person you loved remains in you, your thoughts, your memories, and the positive impact they had on your own life.

COPING WITH GRIEVING AS A TEENAGER

Grief is difficult and confusing. It doesn't matter how old you are; it can be difficult to get through it. Although it can be difficult to deal with, the result can help you move on to a better future. How do you tell if you are grieving? Are there any things teens can do? This chapter will discuss how teenagers can cope with grief and provide some helpful tips.

Teenagers can find it difficult to grieve. It cannot be easy to understand and deal with the situation. Many young people give up on their grief too quickly, not understanding why they feel the way they do.

TEENAGER COMES WITH YOUR GRIEF

The grief and loss that comes with the death of a loved one can be very deep. Without the death of a loved one, you might feel angry, sad, or even lost. It may take some time to accept what has happened. For comfort and support, be patient with yourself.

Teens who have lost a loved one need to understand that there are many ways to grieve. There are helpful and not-so-helpful ways of grieving. You don't have to hold on to your feelings or resort to destructive coping strategies like drinking, substance abuse, or other antisocial or high-risk behaviors. Instead, you can find constructive ways to express what you feel.

The first reaction to loss or death is usually denial, shock, and sadness. The next stage is anger, guilt, and depression, followed by acceptance. These emotions are all normal, and you can feel them all. You may feel multiple emotions and be unable to accept that your loved one is gone. It is possible to be angry about losing a close friend or family member. It is important not to rush through these stages or let yourself get into anger or depression because you refuse to accept what has happened.

1. Do not pretend to be okay if you aren't okay

People can feel depressed when dealing with grief. Don't try to pretend that you're fine to cover up how awful you are. You should inform your family and friends immediately if you feel unwell to the point where you're experiencing depression.

People can feel depressed when dealing with grief. Don't try to pretend that you're fine to cover up how awful you are. Tell your family and friends if you feel unwell to the point where you suffer from depression as soon as possible. Get help

Reach out to someone if this is a problem affecting your school or home. Not only do you need to grieve, but you also need to deal with any other issues that might be coming up.

Reach out to someone if this is something that is affecting you at home or school. Not only do you need to grieve, but you also need to deal with any other issues that might be coming up.

2. Ask questions!

You may be wondering if there's more to grieving than you think. Asking these questions to someone who cares or a professional counselor/therapist is a good idea.

Feeling confused, angry, and sad is normal when you're grieving. These emotions are normal and will pass. This will give you a chance to heal. You will soon see your parents again, and you can start to smile and share your most memorable memories.

3. Participate in rituals

   Funerals and memorial services are great times to get together. They can be a comfort to those who are struggling through the first days. They can be used to remember the deceased. It can be comforting to be with people who know your loved one.

4. It's a good idea to talk about it whenever you can.

   People may want to share their grief or their feelings. Sometimes people don't want to talk. That's OK, too. Nobody should be forced to speak. You can express yourself if you don't feel like speaking. A journal is a good place to start a journal. You can also write a poem, song, or a tribute photo about a loved one. This can be done for your personal use or shared with others.

5. Keep your memories safe.

   Do something to honor someone you love. Plant a tree. Participate in a charity walk or run. Create a memorial box or folder with reminders about the deceased. Include mementos, photos, quotes, or whatever you choose. Write a letter to the person if you wish. You might write your thoughts and feelings in it. Some people write a gratitude letter. This is a way to express gratitude for your loved one's contribution to your life. Keep living the good qualities they encouraged in you as a way of honoring them. You can overcome difficult times with love, gratitude, and meaningful actions.

6. You can re-enter the world at your own pace

It can be very difficult to keep up with the pace of change in the world. There are many challenges to overcome, such as re-entering social media communities, returning to school, and helping others to understand your needs. You may initially find it overwhelming to be in noisy or crowded places. As we become more aware of what is beneficial and what isn't, our grief will lessen over time. You might find that taking your dog on a walk, attending a yoga class nearby, or planting a garden can help you slowly reemerge.

7. Finding support for bereavement

After the death of a loved one, it can take time to adjust. It helps to have lots of support. Support can be provided by family members, friends, and adult mentors. Support groups, therapists, grief counselors, and therapists can also be helpful. Ask your parents, school counselors, or faith leaders for help. It is possible to offer support to others. Talking to others about your grief can help you get through a bereavement. It is up to you to decide whom to talk to about your feelings. Sometimes, the most unlikely person can offer the greatest support. You may find it helpful to talk to someone in your family if you have lost a loved one. They will likely understand what you are feeling.

A close friend can listen and be supportive even if they haven't been through it.

There are many other resources for advice and support, such as:

- Websites and blogs, such as Hope Again, which is a website for young people who are going through a loss, where you can read others' experiences and add your own.
- Talk to your doctor if you are having trouble coping or feel depressed.
- Talk to a tutor or teacher - If you have difficulty with exams or coursework, you might be distracted by other things or feel uneasy.

DEALING WITH GUILT

Nobody ever feels completely guiltless. They are not human if they feel guilty. Guilt can make it difficult for loved ones to grieve, and guilt can make them feel guilty. Guilt can overwhelm you with pain, making you feel like your head is in water.

This chapter will provide some helpful tips for dealing with guilt following the death of a loved one or other negative events.

Tip 1: Time heals all wounds

According to most people, time is the greatest healer. This is especially true when it comes to guilt or grief. It does not mean you are free from feelings about your loss. All wounds can be healed with time. Give yourself some time and patience. Your mind will stop running around in circles about your loss or the guilt you feel. While it may not make the loss completely disappear, it will help you deal with it better.

Tip 2: Express your emotions

It is important to let your emotions out and not keep them inside. This will help you manage guilt. You will feel confused and sad if you have lost a close friend. Although you may not be able to understand the circumstances surrounding their death or how they got there, you will feel sad and confused. You can express your emotions because guilt will grow depending on how long you take to deal with it. It doesn't mean you should not deal with it quickly or even later if it makes you feel the need to. It is important to take small steps and not rush. You should find the most convenient time to do it, and don't force yourself if you aren't ready.

Tip 4: Take a break from school or work if you feel down.

You may find it too difficult to go back to school or work right now. Although it doesn't mean that you have fully processed your loss, going back can help you to forget about it and allow you to try something new. This keeps you busy and prevents your mind from dwelling on the loss and guilt.

Tip 5: Talk to someone who's lost a loved one

Talking with someone who has been through similar experiences can be extremely helpful. They can help you feel better and share their experiences coping with the loss. Although you may not want to talk about the incident, it is important that you are open-minded and willing to share your feelings. This will increase your confidence in dealing with these and other life events.

Tip 6: Keep it in perspective

After the death of a loved one, it is important to keep everything in perspective. Time indeed heals all injuries. Allow yourself to heal, and if necessary, seek professional assistance.

Tip 7: Keep busy

Keep some activities on your agenda, even if you feel like doing nothing. You will feel more positive about the events that have occurred by allowing your mind to wander. You will let your feelings go, so don't hold them back in your mind or heart.

Tip 8: Remember all

It is important to remember what happened but not dwell on the negative aspects. Remember all the positive aspects about your loved ones because these are what makes them unique. You can also remember their strengths and weaknesses, which may help you see the bigger picture and develop better ways to deal with the loss.

Tip 9: Forgive

Find a way to forgive your loved ones if they could forgive you beforeyou died. This is the best thing you can do for your loved one and yourself. This will allow you to let go of all the things that are making it difficult for your life. You can then move on, knowing that you have forgiven yourself for everything.

Tip 10: Learn new facts about the person who has died

Use stories or memories others share to learn more about the deceased or recall more fond memories. This can be done in a group so that everyone can remember different things. You'll be able to recall more positive things about your loved ones if you do this.

Tip 11: Don't feel guilty about not being able to deal with your grief

These tips can help you realize that you don't have to feel guilty about not being able to cope with everything. Everybody grieves at their own pace. As long as you do it healthily and reasonably, it's okay. You are still alive, which matters most to your heart.

GRIEVING IN SCHOOL

It doesn't matter how much a teenager or child grieves, and it's important to remember that they will still go to school. It is difficult to imagine how it will be for them to leave home with a healing heart. For grieving teens and children, a new school year can be difficult.

Parents and caregivers can feel many emotions when sending a grieving child back to school. Parents want their children safe and may be concerned about their grieving child moving out of their home and into an environment that is less secure and less understanding.

While children and teens might long for a normal school day and the safety that comes with it, they may find that their peers often cannot understand the conflicts and confusion caused by the death. Due to the different school experiences caused by the pandemic, children or teens might find themselves with their peers for the first time since the death of their loved one. There is a lot to be worried about, such as who will know what, how it will be received, and what other people will think.

School counselors, administrators, and school teachers might also find themselves in a position to help grieving students. School staff may have also experienced grief during the pandemic or in the summer, and they are trying to help students cope with their feelings and create a supportive and safe environment.

There are no simple answers. Each child is unique, and every situation is different. We want to share some important tips as we transition back to school.

Communicate directly with the school.

A successful transition to school requires good communication between the home of a grieving child/teen and the school. Bereaved children and teens need to know that school staff know about the death and can offer support. It is important to plan ahead to ensure that the student or teen's teacher and administrator have clear guidance for support. Talking to your child or teenager about what the school knows is a good idea. Having them talk to you before or at the start of school is also a good idea so they know whom to call if they need help.

Accept the loss.

Do not pretend that nothing has changed or happened if you support a grieving child/teen. Do not tell the child or teenager to "get over it" or "move forward." It is a life-changing event. Recognizing that you have learned about death is important and can often be one of the best things you can do. Although it may seem like small gestures to say the name of the deceased and continue asking questions about their life, these important acts are vital. Children and teens might not wish to see this in public or too often. While these words and actions help the grieving person to maintain their connection with the deceased, they also allow the student to take part in and honor his or her grief journey. Every child and teenager is unique, so that privacy may be required depending on the circumstances of the death, family circumstances, or individual personality.

Listen carefully.

Children and teens require the trust and stability of all adults, including teachers and parents. Adults should be open to the feelings of a child or teenager after death. Pay attention to what the student has to say. Adults often rush to connect with grieving teens or children by saying things that could make them feel more isolated or hurt. Saying things such as "I understand how you feel," "It could get worse," or "Everything happens because of a reason" can negate their feelings. This is because it makes assumptions about the feelings and beliefs of the person without allowing them to express their own experiences. Instead, listen to the grieving person without trying to fix or remove it. Sometimes children don't want to speak at school. It cannot be easy to balance checking in and letting the child/teen lead, but it is necessary.

Adjust expectations.

Students returning to school following a death might have difficulty with schoolwork. Students who have difficulty concentrating may struggle to do their schoolwork. The inability to concentrate may also impact the student's ability to complete assignments on schedule or at all. These are common symptoms of grief. Talk to your child's or teen's teachers to find the best way to help. This may be a long time for an assignment or a different type of assignment.

Create routines and boundaries.

There may also be behavioral changes in addition to academic matters. Students may engage in harmful or disruptive behaviors or act out. Some students might be quieter and reserved, while others may be more focused and engaged in their work. Although expectations may need to be modified to make a grieving student successful, rules still matter. The rules are still important for a grieving child or teenager. They provide safety, stability, and a sense that there is order and limits. Adults who support grieving teens and children should ensure that they balance flexibility with clear rules and consequences. All significant behavior changes should be noticed at school and home.

These are only suggestions and tips. Each grief journey is different and presents its challenges. I hope you find a rhythm that works for you.

CONCLUSION

It is normal to experience grief. Teens don't "get over" grief but learn to accept it. Teenagers can experience loss in different stages of their lives, so even though it is difficult, the first and second years are particularly hard.

Emotions can resurface through memories and what-if contemplation on special days or important events. The normal development of teenagers involves integrating what they have learned from their loss into their current developmental stage.

The teenage years can be turbulent. Teens who have lost a family member or friend can experience more turmoil. As they age into adulthood, their grief will change as they experience the seasons.

www.ingramcontent.com/pod-product-compliance
Lightning Source LLC
Chambersburg PA
CBHW061201040426

42445CB00013B/1774